The Man with the Hoe

AND OTHER POEMS

By

EDWIN MARKHAM

NEW YORK
DOUBLEDAY & McCLURE COMPANY
1899

Press of J. J. Little & Co.
Astor Place, New York

TO

EDMUND CLARENCE STEDMAN

FIRST TO HAIL AND CAUTION ME

Prefatory Note

Many of these poems have appeared in *Scribner's*, *The Century*, *The Atlantic*, and the San Francisco *Examiner*, and my thanks are due them for permission to republish.

EDWIN MARKHAM.

OAKLAND, CALIFORNIA.

The Man with the Hoe

The Contents

The Contents

The Contents

The Man with the Hoe

Written after seeing Millet's World-Famous Painting

God made man in His own image,
in the image of God made He him.—*Genesis*.

Bowed by the weight of centuries he leans
Upon his hoe and gazes on the ground,
The emptiness of ages in his face,
And on his back the burden of the world.
Who made him dead to rapture and despair,
A thing that grieves not and that never
    hopes,
Stolid and stunned, a brother to the ox?
Who loosened and let down this brutal
    jaw?
Whose was the hand that slanted back this
    brow?
Whose breath blew out the light within this
    brain?

Is this the Thing the Lord God made and
    gave
To have dominion over sea and land;
To trace the stars and search the heavens
    for power;
To feel the passion of Eternity?
Is this the Dream He dreamed who shaped
    the suns
And pillared the blue firmament with light?
Down all the stretch of Hell to its last gulf
There is no shape more terrible than this—
More tongued with censure of the world's
    blind greed—
More filled with signs and portents for the
    soul—
More fraught with menace to the universe.

What gulfs between him and the seraphim!
Slave of the wheel of labor, what to him
Are Plato and the swing of Pleiades?
What the long reaches of the peaks of song,
The rift of dawn, the reddening of the
    rose?

Through this dread shape the suffering ages
    look;
Time's tragedy is in that aching stoop;
Through this dread shape humanity betrayed,
Plundered, profaned and disinherited,
Cries protest to the Judges of the World,
A protest that is also prophecy.

O masters, lords and rulers in all lands,
Is this the handiwork you give to God,
This monstrous thing distorted and soul-
    quenched?
How will you ever straighten up this shape;
Touch it again with immortality;
Give back the upward looking and the light;
Rebuild in it the music and the dream;
Make right the immemorial infamies,
Perfidious wrongs, immedicable woes?

O masters, lords and rulers in all lands,
How will the Future reckon with this Man?
How answer his brute question in that hour
When whirlwinds of rebellion shake the
    world?

How will it be with kingdoms and with
    kings—
With those who shaped him to the thing he
    is—
When this dumb Terror shall reply to God,
After the silence of the centuries?

A Look into the Gulf

I looked one night, and there Semiramis,
With all her mourning doves about her head,
Sat rocking on an ancient road of Hell,
Withered and eyeless, chanting to the moon
Snatches of song they sang to her of old
Upon the lighted roofs of Nineveh.
And then her voice rang out with rattling
    laugh :
"The bugles ! they are crying back again—
Bugles that broke the nights of Babylon,
And then went crying on through Nineveh.

.   .   .   .

Stand back, ye trembling messengers of ill !
Women, let go my hair : I am the Queen,
A whirlwind and a blaze of swords to quell
Insurgent cities.   Let the iron tread
Of armies shake the earth.   Look, lofty
    towers :

Assyria goes by upon the wind!"
And so she babbles by the ancient road,
While cities turned to dust upon the Earth
Rise through her whirling brain to live again—
Babbles all night, and when her voice is dead
Her weary lips beat on without a sound.

Brotherhood

The crest and crowning of all good,
Life's final star, is Brotherhood;
For it will bring again to Earth
Her long-lost Poesy and Mirth;
Will send new light on every face,
A kingly power upon the race.
And till it come, we men are slaves,
And travel downward to the dust of graves.

Come, clear the way, then, clear the way :
Blind creeds and kings have had their day.
Break the dead branches from the path;
Our hope is in the aftermath—
Our hope is in heroic men,
Star-led to build the world again.
To this Event the ages ran :
Make way for Brotherhood—make way for
    Man.

Song of the Followers of Pan

Our bursting bugles blow apart
  The gates of cities as we go ;
We bring the music of the heart
  From secret wells in Lillimo'.

We break in music on the morns—
  Sing of the flower to stirring roots ;
Apollo's cry is in the horns,
  And Hermes' whisper in the flutes.

We come with laughter to the Earth,
  And lightly stir the heading wheat :
Our God is Poesy and Mirth,
  And loves the noise of woodland feet.

When dancers beat the air to sound,
  After the time of yellow sheaves,
He stops to watch the merry round,
  His pleased face looking through the
    leaves.

Little Brothers of the Ground

Little ants in leafy wood,
Bound by gentle Brotherhood,
While ye gaily gather spoil,
Men are ground by the wheel of toil;
While ye follow Blessed Fates,
Men are shriveled up with hates.
Yes, they eat the wayside dust,
While their souls are gnawed by rust.

Ye are fraters in your hall,
Gay and chainless, great and small;
All are toilers in the field,
All are sharers in the yield.
But we mortals plot and plan
How to grind the fellow-man;
Glad to find him in a pit,
If we get some gain of it.
So with us, the sons of Time,
Labor is a kind of crime,

For the toilers have the least,
While the idlers lord the feast.
Yes, our workers they are bound,
Pallid captives to the ground ;
Jeered by traitors, fooled by knaves,
Till they stumble into graves.

How appears to tiny eyes
All this wisdom of the wise ?

Wail of the Wandering Dead

Death, too, is a chimera and betrays,
    And yet they promised we should enter
        rest;
Death is as empty as the cup of days,
    And bitter milk is in her wintry breast.

There is no worth in any world to come,
    Nor any in the world we left behind;
And what remains of all our masterdom ?—
    Only a cry out of the crumbling mind.

We played all comers at the old Gray Inn,
    But played the King of Players to our
        cost.
We played Him fair and had no chance to
        win :
    The dice of God were loaded and we lost.

We wander, wander, and the nights come
    down
    With starless darkness and the rush of
      rains ;
We drift as phantoms by the songless town,
    We drift as litter on the windy lanes.

Hope is the fading vision of the heart,
    A mocking spirit throwing up wild hands.
She led us on with music at the start,
    To leave us at dead fountains in the sands.

Now all our days are but a cry for sleep,
    For we are weary of the petty strife.
Is there not somewhere in the endless deep
    A place where we can lose the feel of life ?

Where we can be as senseless as the dust
    The night wind blows about a dried-up
      well ?
Where there is no more labor, no more lust,
    Nor any flesh to feel the Tooth of Hell ?

Our feet are ever sliding, and we seem
  As old and weary as the pyramids.
Come, God of Ages, and dispel the dream,
  Fold the worn hands and close the sinking
    lids.

There is no new road for the dead to take :
  Wild hearts are we among the worlds
    astray—
Wild hearts are we that cannot wholly break,
  But linger on though life has gone away.

We are the sons of Misery and Eld :
  Come, tender Death, with all your hushing
    wings,
And let our broken spirits be dispelled—
  Let dead men sink into the dusk of things.

A Prayer

Teach me, Father, how to go
Softly as the grasses grow;
Hush my soul to meet the shock
Of the wild world as a rock;
But my spirit, propt with power,
Make as simple as a flower.
Let the dry heart fill its cup,
Like a poppy looking up;
Let life lightly wear her crown,
Like a poppy looking down,
When its heart is filled with dew,
And its life begins anew.

Teach me, Father, how to be
Kind and patient as a tree.
Joyfully the crickets croon
Under shady oak at noon;

A Prayer

Beetle, on his mission bent,
Tarries in that cooling tent.
Let me, also, cheer a spot,
Hidden field or garden grot—
Place where passing souls can rest
On the way and be their best.

The Poet

His home is on the heights: to him
Men wage a battle weird and dim,
Life is a mission stern as fate,
And Song a dread apostolate.
The toils of prophecy are his,
To hail the coming centuries—
To ease the steps and lift the load
Of souls that falter on the road.
The perilous music that he hears
Falls from the vortice of the spheres.

He presses on before the race,
And sings out of a silent place.
Like faint notes of a forest bird
On heights afar that voice is heard;
And the dim path he breaks to-day
Will some time be a trodden way.

But when the race comes toiling on
That voice of wonder will be gone—
Be heard on higher peaks afar,
Moved upward with the morning star.

O men of earth, that wandering voice
Still goes the upward way : rejoice !

The Whirlwind Road

The Muses wrapped in mysteries of light
Came in a rush of music on the night;
And I was lifted wildly on quick wings,
And borne away into the deep of things.
The dead doors of my being broke apart;
A wind of rapture blew across the heart;
The inward song of worlds rang still and clear;
I felt the Mystery the Muses fear;
Yet they went swiftening on the ways untrod,
And hurled me breathless at the feet of God.

I felt faint touches of the Final Truth—
Moments of trembling love, moments of youth.
A vision swept away the human wall;
Slowly I saw the meaning of it all—
Meaning of life and time and death and birth,
But can not tell it to the men of Earth.
I only point the way, and they must go
The whirlwind road of song if they would
    know.

The Desire of Nations

And the government shall be upon His shoulder: and His name
shall be called Wonderful, Counsellor, The mighty God, The ever-
lasting Father, The Prince of Peace.—*Isaiah.*

Earth will go back to her lost youth,
And life grow deep and wonderful as truth,
When the wise King out of the nearing
      Heaven comes
To break the spell of long millenniums—
To build with song again
The broken hope of men—
To hush and heroize the world,
Under the flag of Brotherhood unfurled.
And He will come some day :
Already is His star upon the way !
He comes, O world, He comes !
But not with bugle-cry nor roll of doubling
      drums.

Nay, for He comes to loosen and unbind,
To build the lofty purpose in the mind,

To stir the heart's deep chord.   .   .   .
No rude horns parleying, no shock of shields;
Nor as of old the glory of the Lord
To half-awakened shepherds in the fields,
Looking with foolish faces on the rush
Of the Great Splendor, when the pulsing hush
Came o'er the hills, came o'er the heavens afar
Where on their cliff of stars the watching
    seraphs are.

Nor as of old when first the Strong One trod,
The Power of sepulchers—our Risen God!
When on that deathless morning in the dark,
He quit the Garden of the Sepulcher,
Setting the oleander boughs astir,
And pausing at the gate with backward
    hark.—
Nay, nor as when the Hero-King of Heaven
Came with upbraiding to His faint Eleven,
And found the world-way to His bright feet
    barred,
And hopeless then because men's hearts
    were hard.

Nor will He come like carnal kings of old,
With pomp of pilfered gold;
Nor like the pharisees with pride of prayer;
Nor as the stumbling foolish stewards
dream
In tedious argument and milkless creed,
But in the passion of the heart-warm deed
Will come the Man Supreme.
Yea, for He comes to lift the Public Care—
To build on Earth the Vision hung in air.
This is the one fulfillment of His Law—
The one Fact in the mockeries that seem.
This is the Vision that the prophets saw—
The Comrade Kingdom builded in their
dream.

No, not as in that elder day
Comes now the King upon the human way.
He comes with power: His white unfearing
face
Shines through the Social Passion of the
race.
He comes to frame the freedom of the Law,

To touch these men of Earth
With a feeling of life's oneness and its
    worth,
A feeling of its mystery and awe.

And when He comes into the world gone
    wrong,
He will rebuild her beauty with a song.
To every heart He will its own dream be :
One moon has many phantoms in the sea.
Out of the North the norns will cry to
    men :
" Balder the Beautiful has come again !"
The flutes of Greece will whisper from the
    dead :
" Apollo has unveiled his sunbright head!"
The stones of Thebes and Memphis will
    find voice :
" Osiris comes : O tribes of Time, rejoice !"
And social architects who build the State,
Serving the Dream at citadel and gate,
Will hail Him coming through the labor-
    hum.

And glad quick cries will go from man to
    man :
" Lo, He has come, our Christ the Artisan—
The King who loved the lilies, He has
    come ! "

He will arrive, our Counselor and Chief.
And with bleak faces lighted up will come
The earth-worn mothers from their martyr-
    dom,
To tell Him of their grief.
And glad girls caroling from field and town
Will go to meet Him with the labor-crown,
The new crown woven of the heading
    wheat.
And men will sit down at His sacred feet ;
And He will say—the King—
"Come, let us live the poetry we sing ! "
And these, His burning words, will break
    the ban—
Words that will grow to be,
On continent, on sea,
The rallying cry of man. . . .

He comes to make the long injustice right—
Comes to push back the shadow of the
    night,
The gray Tradition full of flint and flaw—
Comes to wipe out the insults to the soul,
The insults of the Few against the Whole,
The insults they make righteous with a law.

Yea, He will bear the Safety of the State,
For in his still and rhythmic steps will be
The power and music of Alcyone,
Who holds the swift heavens in their starry
    fate.
Yea, He will lay on souls the power of
    peace,
And send on kingdoms torn the sense of
    home—
More than the fire of Joy that burned on
    Greece,
More than the light of Law that rose on
    Rome.

The Elf Child

I am a child of the reef and the blowing spray,
  And all my heart goes wildly to the sea.
  I am a changeling : can you follow me
Through hill and hollow on the wind's dim
      way ?
Yes, at the break of a tempestuous day
   They bore me to the land through starless
     storm,
  And laid me in the pillow sweetly warm
And broken by the first one's little stay.

The elf kings found me on an ocean reef,
A lyric child of mystery and grief.
  Then need I tell you why the trembling
    start—
Why in my song the sound of ocean dwells—
Why the quick gladness when the billow
    swells,
  As though remembered voices called the
    heart ?

The Goblin Laugh

When I behold how men and women grind
  And grovel for some place of pomp or
    power,
  To shine and circle through a crumbling
    hour,
Forgetting the large mansions of the mind,
That are the rest and shelter of mankind;
  And when I see them come with wearied
    brains
  Pallid and powerless to enjoy their gains,
I seem to hear a goblin laugh unwind.

And then a memory sends upon its billow
  Thoughts of a singer wise enough to play,
  Who took life as a lightsome holiday:
Oft have I seen him make his arm a pillow,
Drink from his hand, and with a pipe of wil-
    low
  Blow a wild music down a woodland way.

Poetry

She comes like the hush and beauty of the
    night,
  And sees too deep for laughter;
Her touch is a vibration and a light
  From worlds before and after.

A Meeting

Softly she came one twilight from the dead,
    And in the passionate silence of her look
    Was more than man has writ in any book :
And now my thoughts are restless, and a
      dread
Calls them to the Dim Land discomforted ;
    For down the leafy ways her white feet
      took,
    Lightly the newly broken roses shook—
Was it the wind disturbed each rosy head ?

God ! was it joy or sorrow in her face—
    That quiet face ? Had it grown old or
      young ?
    Was it sweet memory or sad that stung
Her voiceless soul to wander from its place?
What do the dead find in the Silence—grace ?
    Or endless grief for which there is no
      tongue ?

Infinite Depths

The little pool, in street or field apart,
   Glasses the deep heavens and the rushing
      storm ;
And into the silent depths of every heart,
   The Eternal throws its awful shadow-form.

A Leaf from the Devil's Jest-Book

Beside the sewing-table chained and bent,
  They stitch for the lady, tyrannous and
      proud—
  For her a wedding-gown, for them a
      shroud;
They stitch and stitch, but never mend the
      rent
Torn in life's golden curtains. Glad Youth
      went,
  And left them alone with Time; and now
      if bowed
  With burdens they should sob and cry
      aloud,—
Wondering, the filled would look from their
      content.

And so this glimmering life at last recedes
  In unknown, endless depths beyond recall;

And what's the worth of all our ancient
    creeds,
  If here at the end of ages this is all—
  A white face floating in the whirling ball,
A dead face plashing in the river reeds?

The Paymaster

There is a sacred Something on all ways—
  Something that watches through the Uni-
    verse ;
One that remembers, reckons and repays,
  Giving us love for love, and curse for
    curse.

The Last Furrow

The Spirit of Earth, with still restoring
    hands,
   'Mid ruin moves, in glimmering chasm
     gropes,
   And mosses mantle and the bright flower
     opes;
But Death the Ploughman wanders in all
    lands,
And to the last of Earth his furrow stands.
   The grave is never hidden; fearful hopes
Follow the dead upon the fading slopes,
   And there wild memories meet upon the
     sands.

When willows fling their banners to the plain,
   When rumor of winds and sound of sudden
    showers

Disturb the dream of winter—all in vain
  The grasses hurry to the graves, the flowers
  Toss their wild torches on their windy
      towers ;
Yet are the bleak graves lonely in the rain.

In the Storm

I huddled close against the mighty cliff.
A sense of safety and of brotherhood
Broke on the heart : the shelter of a rock
Is sweeter than the roofs of all the world.

After Reading Shakspere

Blithe Fancy lightly builds with airy hands
  Or on the edges of the darkness peers,
  Breathless and frightened at the Voice she
      hears :
Imagination (lo ! the sky expands)
Travels the blue arch and Cimmerian
      sands,—
  Homeless on earth, the pilgrim of the
      spheres,
  The rush of light before the hurrying
      years,
The Voice that cries in unfamiliar lands.

Men weigh the moons that flood with eerie
      light
  The dusky vales of Saturn—wood and
      stream ;

But who shall follow on the awful sweep
Of Neptune through the dim and dreadful
    deep?
Onward he wanders in the unknown night,
And we are shadows moving in a dream.

The Hidden Valley

I stray with Ariel and Caliban:
    I know the hill of windy pines—I know
    Where the jay's nest swings in the wild
        gorge below:
Lightly I climb where fallen cedars span
Bright rivers—climb to a valley under ban,
    Where west winds set a thousand bells
        ablow—
    An eerie valley where in the morning
        glow
I hear the music of the pipes of Pan.

Mysterious horns blow by on the still air—
    A satyr steps—a wood-god's dewy notes
    Come faintly from a vale of tossing oats.—
But ho! what white thing in the canyon
        crossed?
Gods! I shall come on Dian unaware,
Look on her fearful beauty and be lost.

The Poets

Some cry of Sappho's lyre, of Saadi's flute,
    Comes back across the waste of mortal
        things :
Men strive and die to reach the Dead Sea
        fruit—
    Only the poets find immortal springs.

Love's Vigil

Love will outwatch the stars, and light the
    skies
    When the last star falls, and the silent
      dark devours;
    God's warrior, he will watch the allotted
      hours,
And conquer with the look of his sad eyes:
He shakes the kingdom of darkness with his
    sighs,
    His quiet sighs, while all the Infernal
      Powers
    Tremble and pale upon their central
      towers,
Lest, haply, his bright universe arise.

All will be well if he have strength to wait,
    Till his lost Pleiad, white and silver-shod,
Regains her place to make the perfect
    Seven;

Then all the worlds will know that Love is
    Fate—
That somehow he is greater even than
    Heaven—
That in the Cosmic Council he is God.

Two at a Fireside

I built a chimney for a comrade old ;
   I did the service not for hope or hire :
And then I traveled on in winter's cold,
   Yet all the day I glowed before the fire.

The Butterfly

O wingèd brother on the harebell, stay—
  Was God's hand very pitiful, the hand
  That wrought thy beauty at a dream's de-
    mand?
Yes, knowing I love so well the flowery way,
He did not fling me to the world astray—
  He did not drop me to the weary sand,
  But bore me gently to a leafy land:
Tinting my wings, He gave me to the day.

Oh, chide no more my doubting, my despair!
  I will go back now to the world of men.
Farewell, I leave thee to the world of air,
  Yet thou hast girded up my heart again;
For He that framed the impenetrable plan,
And keeps His word with thee, will keep with
  man.

To William Watson

After reading "The Purple East."

That hour you put the wreath of England by
  To shake her guilty heart with song sub-
    lime,
The mighty Muse that watches from the sky
  Laid on your head the larger wreath of
    Time.

Keats A-Dying

Often of that Last Hour I lie and think;
   I see thee, Keats, nearing the Deathway
      dim—
See Severn in his noiseless hurry, him
Who leaned above thee fading on the brink.
   .   .   .   .   :   .   .

What is that wild light through the window
   chink?
   Is it the burning feet of cherubim?
   Or is it the white moon on western rim—
Saint Agnes' moon beginning now to sink?

How did Death come—with sounds of water-
   stir?
   With forms of beauty breaking at the lips?
With field pipes and the scent of blowing fir?
   Or came it hurrying like a last eclipse,
Sweeping the world away like gossamer,
   Blotting the moon, the mountains, and the
      ships?

Man

Out of the deep and endless universe
There came a greater Mystery, a Shape,
A Something sad, inscrutable, august—
One to confront the worlds and question
    them.

The Cricket

The twilight is the morning of his day.
   While Sleep drops seaward from the fad-
      ing shore,
   With purpling sail and dip of silver oar,
He cheers the shadowed time with roun-
      delay,
Until the dark east softens into gray.
   Now as the noisy hours are coming—hark!
   His song dies gently—it is growing dark—
His night, with its one star, is on its way!

Faintly the light breaks over the blowing
      oats—
   Sleep, little brother, sleep: I am astir.
   We worship Song, and servants are of her—
I in the bright hours, thou in shadow-time:
Lead thou the starlit night with merry notes,
And I will lead the clamoring day with
      rhyme.

In High Sierras

There at a certain hour of the deep night,
A gray cliff with a demon face comes up,
Wrinkled and old, behind the peaks, and with
An anxious look peers at the Zodiac.

The Wharf of Dreams

Strange wares are handled on the wharves
    of sleep:
  Shadows of shadows pass, and many a
    light
  Flashes a signal fire across the night;
Barges depart whose voiceless steersmen
    keep
Their way without a star upon the deep;
  And from lost ships, homing with ghostly
    crews,
  Come cries of incommunicable news,
While cargoes pile the piers, a moon-white
    heap—

Budgets of dream-dust, merchandise of song,
Wreckage of hope and packs of ancient
    wrong,

Nepenthes gathered from a secret strand,
Fardels of heartache, burdens of old sins,
Luggage sent down from dim ancestral inns,
And bales of fantasy from No-Man's Land.

To Louise Michel

I cannot take your road, Louise Michel,
   Priestess of Pity and of Vengeance—no:
   Down that amorphous gulf I cannot go—
That gulf of Anarchy whose pit is Hell.
Yet, sister, though my first word is farewell,
   Remember that I know your hidden woe;
   Have felt the grief that rends you blow on
      blow;
Have knelt beside you in the murky cell.

You never followed hate (let this atone)
Nor knew the wrongs of others from your
      own:
   Wild was the road, but Love has always
      led:
So I am silent where I cannot praise;
And here now at the parting of the ways,
   I lay a still hand lightly on your head.

Shepherd Boy and Nereid

Ah, once of old in some forgotten tongue,
  Forgotten land, I was a shepherd boy,
  And you a Nereid, a wingèd joy :
On through the dawn-bright peaks our
    bodies swung,
And flower-soft lyrics by immortals sung
  Fell from their unseen pinnacles in
    air :
  God looked from Heaven that hour, for
    you were fair,
And I a poet, and the star was young.

You'd heard my woodland pipe and left the
    sea—
  Your hair blown gold and all your body
    white—
Had left the ocean-girls to follow me.

We joined the hill-nymphs in their joyous
    flight,
And you laughed lightly to the sea, and sent
Quick glances flashing through me as I
    went.

A Song at the Start

Oh, down the quick river our galley is
    going,
  With a sound in the cordage, a beam on
    the sail :
The wind of the canyon our loose hair is
    blowing,
  And the clouds of the morning are glad
    of the gale.

Around the swift prow little billows are
    breaking,
  And flinging their foam in a glory of
    light ;
Now the shade of a rock on the river is
    shaking,
  And a wave leaping upward grows sud-
    denly white.

The weight of the whole world is light as a
    feather,
  And the peaks rise in silence and westerly
    flee :
Oh, the world and the poet are singing to-
    gether,
  And from the far cliff comes a sound of
    the sea.

My Comrade

I never build a song by night or day,
  Of breaking ocean or of blowing whin,
But in some wondrous unexpected way,
  Like light upon a road, my Love comes in.

And when I go at night upon the hill,
  My heart is lifted on mysterious wings :
My Love is there to strengthen and to still,
  For she can take away the dread of things.

A Lyric of the Dawn

Alone I list
In the leafy tryst;
Silent the woodlands in their starry sleep—
Silent the phantom wood in waters deep:
No footfall of a wind along the pass
Startles a harebell—stirs a blade of grass.
Yonder the wandering weeds,
Enchanted in the light,
'Stand in the gusty hollows, still and white;
Yonder are plumy reeds,
Dusking the border of the clear lagoon;
Far off the silver clifts
Hang in ethereal light below the moon;
Far off the ocean lifts,
Tossing its billows in the misty beam,
And shore-lines whiten, silent as a dream:

71

I hark for the bird, and all the hushed hills
    harken :
This is the valley : here the branches darken
    The silver-lighted stream.

    Hark—
That rapture in the leafy dark !
Who is it shouts upon the bough aswing,
Waking the upland and the valley under ?
What carols, like the blazon of a king,
    Fill all the dawn with wonder ?
      Oh, hush,
It is the thrush,
In the deep and woody glen !
Ah, thus the gladness of the gods was
    sung,
    When the old Earth was young ;
    That rapture rang,
When the first morning on the mountains
    sprang :
And now he shouts, and the world is young
    again !

Carol, my king,
On your bough aswing!
Thou art not of these evil days—
Thou art a voice of the world's lost youth:
Oh, tell me what is duty—what is truth—
How to find God upon these hungry ways;
Tell of the golden prime,
When bird and beast could make a man their
friend;
When men beheld swift deities descend,
Before the race was left alone with Time,
Homesick on Earth, and homeless to the end;
Before great Pan was dead,
Before the naiads fled;
When maidens white with dark eyes shy and
bold,
With peals of laughter on the peaks of gold,
Startled the still dawn—
Shone in upon the mountains and were gone,
Their voices fading silverly in depths of for-
ests old.

Sing of the wonders of their woodland ways,
Before the weird earth-hunger of these days,

When there was rippling mirth,
When justice was on Earth,
And light and grandeur of the Golden Age;
When never a heart was sad,
When all from king to herdsman had
A penny for a wage.
Ah, that old time has faded to a dream—
The moon's fair face is broken in the stream;
Yet shout and carol on, O bird, and let
The exiled race not utterly forget;
Publish thy revelation on the lawns—
Sing ever in the dark ethereal dawns;
Sometime, in some sweet year,
These stormy souls, these men of Earth may
hear.

But hark again,
From the secret glen,
That voice of rapture and ethereal youth
Now laden with despair.
Forbear, O bird, forbear:
Is life not terrible enough forsooth?
Cease, cease the mystic song—

A Lyric of the Dawn

No more, no more, the passion and the pain:
It wakes my life to fret against the chain;
It makes me think of all the agèd wrong—
Of joy and the end of joy and the end of
    all—
Of souls on Earth, and souls beyond recall.
  Ah, ah, that voice again!
It makes me think of all these restless men,
Called into time—their progress and their
    goal;
  And now, oh now, it sends into my soul
Dreams of a love that might have been for
    me—
That might have been—and now can never
    be.

  Tell me no more of these—
  Tell me of trancèd trees;
(The ghosts, the memories, in pity spare)
Show me the leafy home of the wild bees;
Show me the snowy summits dim in air;
  Tell me of things afar
In valleys silent under moon and star:

Dim hollows hushed with night,
The lofty cedars misty in the light,
   Wild clusters of the vine,
   Wild odors of the pine,
The eagle's eyrie lifted to the moon—
High places where on quiet afternoon
A shadow swiftens by, a thrilling scream
Startles the cliff, and dies across the wood-
    land to a dream.

    Ha, now
  He springs from the bough,
  It flickers—he is lost!
  Out of the copse he sprang;
This is the floating briar where he tossed:
The leaves are yet atremble where he sang.
  Here a long vista opens—look!
  This is the way he took,
Through the pale poplars by the pond:
Hark! he is shouting in the field beyond.
  Ho, there he goes
  Through the alder close!

He leaves me here behind him in his flight,
And yet my heart goes with him out of
 sight!
 What whispered spell
Of Faëry calls me on from dell to dell?
I hear the voice—it wanders in a dream—
Now in the grove, now on the hill, now on
 the fading stream.

 Lead on—you know the way—
  Lead on to Arcady,
O'er fields asleep; by river bank abrim;
Down leafy ways, dewy and cool and dim;
By dripping rocks, dark dwellings of the
 gnome,
Where hurrying waters dash their crests to
 foam.
 I follow where you lead,
Down winding paths, across the flowery mead,
Down silent hollows where the woodbine
 blows,
Up water-courses scented by the rose.

A Lyric of the Dawn

I follow the wandering voice—
I follow, I rejoice,
I fade away into the Age of Gold—
We two together lost in forest old.—
O ferny and thymy paths, O fields of Aidenn,
Canyons and cliffs by mortal feet untrod!
O souls that weary and are heavy laden,
    Here is the peace of God!

Lo! now the clamoring hours are on the
    way:
Faintly the pine tops redden in the ray;
From vale to vale fleet-footed rumors run,
With sudden apprehension of the sun;
    A light wind stirs
The filmy tops of delicate dim firs,
  And on the river border blows,
Breaking the shy bud softly to a rose.
  Sing out, O throstle, sing:
  I follow on, my king:
Lead me forever through the crimson dawn—
  Till the world ends, lead me on!

Ho there! he shouts again—he sways—and
   now,
  Upspringing from the bough,
Flashing a glint of dew upon the ground,
  Without a sound
He drops into a valley and is gone!

Joy of the Morning

I hear you, little bird,
Shouting aswing above the broken wall.
Shout louder yet: no song can tell it all.
Sing to my soul in the deep still wood:
'Tis wonderful beyond the wildest word:
I'd tell it, too, if I could.

Oft when the white, still dawn
Lifted the skies and pushed the hills apart,
I've felt it like a glory in my heart—
(The world's mysterious stir)
But had no throat like yours, my bird,
Nor such a listener.

The Waning Lamp

Once, I remember, the world was young;
The rills rejoiced with a silver tongue;
The field-lark sat in the wheat and sang;
The thrush's shout in the woodland rang;
The cliffs and the perilous sands afar
Were softened to mist by the morning star;
For Youth was with me (I know it now!),
And a light shone out from his wreathèd
    brow.
He turned the fields to enchanted ground,
He touched the rains with a dreamy sound.

But alas, he vanished, and Time appeared,
The Spirit of Ages, old and weird.
He crushed and scattered my beamy wings;
He dragged me forth from the court of
    kings;

The Waning Lamp

He gave me doubt and a bloom of beard,
This Spirit of Ages, old and weird.
The wonder went from the field of corn,
The glory died on the craggy horn;
And suddenly all was strange and gray,
And the rocks came out on the trodden way.

I hear no more the wild thrush sing:
He is silent now on the peach aswing.
Something is gone from the house of mirth—
Something is gone from the hills of Earth.
Time hurries me on with a wizard hand;
He turns the Earth to a homeless land;
He stays my life with a stingy breath,
And darkens its depths with foreknowledge
    of death;
Calls memories back on their path apace;
Sends desperate thoughts to the soul's dim
    place.

Time murders our youth and the griefs
    begin,
As he pushes us on to the windowless inn.

A Satyr Song

I know by the stir of the branches
   The way she went ;
And at times I can see where a stem
   Of the grass is bent.
She's the secret and light of my life,
   She allures to elude ;
But I follow the spell of her beauty
   Whatever the mood.

I have followed all night in the hills,
   And my breath is deep,
But she flies on before like a voice
   In the vale of sleep.
I follow the print of her feet
   In the wild river bed,
And lo, she calls gleefully down
   From a cliff overhead.

A Cry in the Night

Wail, wail, wail,
  For the fleering world goes down:
Into the song of the poet pale
  Mixes the laugh of the clown.

Grim, grim, grim,
  Is the road we go to the dead;
Yet we must on, for a Something dim
  Pushes the soul ahead.

Where, where, where,
  Through the dust and shadow of things
Will the fleeing Fates with their wild
    manes bear
  These tribes of slaves and kings?

Fays

One secret night, I stood where ocean pours
Eternal waters on the yellow shores,
And saw the drift of fays that Prosper saw :
(Their feet had no more sound than blow-
    ing straw.)
And little hands held light in little hands
They chased a fleeing billow down the sands,
But turned in the nick o' time, and mad with
    glee
Raced back again before the swelling sea.

In Death Valley

There came gray stretches of volcanic plains,
Bare, lone and treeless, then a bleak lone
    hill,
Like to the dolorous hill that Dobell saw.
Around were heaps of ruins piled between
The Burn o' Sorrow and the Water o' Care;
And from the stillness of the down-crushed
    walls
One pillar rose up dark against the moon.
There was a nameless Presence everywhere;
In the gray soil there was a purple stain,
And the gray reticent rocks were dyed with
    blood—
Blood of a vast unknown Calamity.
It was the mark of some ancestral grief—
Grief that began before the ancient Flood.

Business

Just then the branches lightly stirred. . . .
See, out o' the apple boughs a bird
Bursts music-mad into the blue abyss:
Rothschild would give his gold for this—
The wealth of nations, if he knew:
(And find a profit in the business, too.)

" Follow Me "

O friend, we never choose the better part,
Until we set the Cross up in the heart.
I know I can not live until I die—
Till I am nailed upon it wild and high,
And sleep in the tomb for a full three days
    dead,
With angels at the feet and at the head.
But then in a great brightness I shall rise
To walk with stiller feet below the skies.

In Poppy Fields

Here the poppy hosts assemble:
How they startle, how they tremble!
All their royal hoods unpinned
Blow out lightly in the wind.

Men that in the cities grind,
Come before the heart is blind.
Here is gold to labor for;
Here is pillage worth a war!

The Joy of the Hills

I ride on the mountain tops, I ride;
I have found my life and am satisfied.
Onward I ride in the blowing oats,
Checking the field-lark's rippling notes—
  Lightly I sweep
  From steep to steep:
Over my head through the branches high
Come glimpses of a rushing sky;
The tall oats brush my horse's flanks;
Wild poppies crowd on the sunny banks;
A bee booms out of the scented grass;
A jay laughs with me as I pass.

I ride on the hills, I forgive, I forget
  Life's hoard of regret—
  All the terror and pain
  Of the chafing chain.

Grind on, O cities, grind:
I leave you a blur behind.
I am lifted elate—the skies expand:
Here the world's heaped gold is a pile of
　　sand.
Let them weary and work in their narrow
　　walls:
I ride with the voices of waterfalls!

I swing on as one in a dream—I swing
Down the airy hollows, I shout, I sing!
The world is gone like an empty word:
My body's a bough in the wind, my heart a
　　bird!

The Invisible Bride

The low-voiced girls that go
   In gardens of the Lord,
Like flowers of the field they grow
   In sisterly accord.

Their whispering feet are white
   Along the leafy ways;
They go in whirls of light
   Too beautiful for praise.

And in their band forsooth
   Is one to set me free—
The one that touched my youth—
   The one God gave to me.

She kindles the desire
   Whereby the gods survive—
The white ideal fire
   That keeps my soul alive.

The Invisible Bride

Now at the wondrous hour,
  She leaves her star supreme,
And comes in the night's still **power**,
  To touch me with a dream.

Sibyl of mystery
  On roads unknown to men,
Softly she comes to me,
  And goes to God again.

The Valley

I know a valley in the summer hills,
Haunted by little winds and daffodils;
Faint footfalls and soft shadows pass at noon;
Noiseless, at night, the clouds assemble there;
And ghostly summits hang below the moon—
Dim visions lightly swung in silent air.

The Climb of Life

There's a feel of all things flowing,
  And no power of Earth can bind them;
There's a sense of all things growing,
And through all their forms a glowing
  Of the shaping souls behind them.

And the break of beauty heightens
  With the swiftening of the motion,
And the soul behind it lightens,
As a gleam of splendor whitens
  From a running wave of ocean.

See the still hand of the Shaper,
  Moving in the dusk of being:
Burns at first a misty taper,
Like the moon in veil of vapor,
  When the rack of night is fleeing.

In the stone a dream is sleeping,
    Just a tinge of life, a tremor;
In the tree a soul is creeping—
Last, a rush of angels sweeping
    With the skies beyond the dreamer.

So the Lord of Life is flinging
    Out a splendor that conceals Him:
And the God is softly singing
And on secret ways is winging,
    Till the rush of song reveals Him.

The Tragedy

Oh, the fret of the brain,
  And the wounds and the worry ;
Oh, the thought of love and the thought of
    death—
  And the soul in its silent hurry.

But the stars break above,
  And the fields flower under ;
And the tragical life of man goes on,
  Surrounded by beauty and wonder.

Divine Vision

Can it be the Master knows
How the Cosmic Blossom blows?

Yes, at times the Lord of Light
Breaks forth wonderful and white,
And he strikes a chorded lyre
In a rush of whirlwind fire;
And He sees before Him pass
Souls and planets in a glass;
And within the music hears
All the motions of all spheres,
All the whispers of all feet,
Cries of triumph and retreat,
Songs of systems and of souls,
Circling to their mighty goals.

So the Lord of Light beholds
How the Cosmic Flower unfolds.

Midsummer Noon

Yonder a workman, under the cool bridge,
Resting at mid-day, watches the glancing
    midge,
While twinkling lights and murmurs of the
    stream
Pass into the dim fabric of his dream :
The misty hollows and the drowsy ridge—
How like an airy fantasy they seem.

One Life, One Law

What do we know—what need we know
Of the great world to which we go?
We peer into the tomb, and hark:
Its walls are dim, its doors are dark.

Be still, O mourning heart, nor seek
To make the tongueless silence speak:
Be still, be strong, nor wish to find
Their way who leave the world behind—
Voices and forms forever gone
Into the darkness of the dawn.

What is their wisdom, clear and deep?—
That as men sow they surely reap,—
That every thought, that every deed,
Is sown into the soul for seed.
They have no word we do not know,—
Nor yet the cherubim aglow
With God: we know that virtue saves,—
They know no more beyond the graves.

Griefs

The rains of winter scourged the weald,
For days they darkened on the field :
Now, where the wings of winter beat,
The poppies ripple in the wheat.

And pitiless griefs came thick and fast—
Life's bough was naked in the blast—
Till silently amid the gloom
They blew the wintry heart to bloom.

An Old Road

A host of poppies, a flight of swallows;
A flurry of rain, and a wind that follows
Shepherds the leaves in the sheltered hol-
    lows,
    For the forest is shaken and thinned.

Over my head are the firs for rafter;
The crows blow south, and my heart goes
    after;
I kiss my hands to the world with laughter—
    Is it Aidenn or mystical Ind?

Oh, the whirl of the fields in the windy
    weather!
How the barley breaks and blows together!
Oh, glad is the free bird afloat on the
    heather—
    Oh, the whole world is glad of the wind!

The New-Comers

Two swallows—each preening a long glossy
    feather;
Now they gossip and dart through the sil-
    very weather;
Oh, praise to the Highest—two lovers to-
    gether—
    Free, free in the fathomless world of air.

No fate to oppose and no fortune to sunder;
Blue sky overhead—green sky breaking un-
    der;
And their home on the cliff in the midst of
    the wonder,
    With never a thought of the morrow
    there.

Music

It is the last appeal to man—
Voice crying since the world began;
The cry of the Ideal—cry
To aspirations that would die.
The last appeal! in it is heard
The pathos of the final word.

Voice tender and heroical—
Imperious voice that knoweth well
To wreck the reasonings of years,
To strengthen rebel hearts with tears.

Fay Song

My life is a dream—a dream
In the moon's cool beam ;
Some day I shall wake and desire
A touch of the infinite fire.
But now 'tis enough that I be
In the light of the sea ;
Enough that I climb with the cloud
When the winds of the morning are loud ;
Enough that I fade with the stars
When the door of the East unbars.

The Old Earth

How will it be if there we find no traces—
There in the Golden Heaven—if we find
No memories of the old Earth left behind,
No visions of familiar forms and faces—
Reminders of old voices and old places?
Yet could we bear it if it should remind?

Divine Adventure

At times a youth (so whispered legend tells),
Like Hylas, stoops to drink
By forest-hidden brink,
And fair hands draw him down to darkened
    wells;
Fair hands that hold him fast
With laughter at the last
Have power to draw him lightly down to be
In elfin chambers under the gray sea.

And I, O men of Earth, I too,
When dawn was at the dew,
Was drawn as Hylas downward and beheld
Spirits of youth and eld—
Was swung down endless caverns to the
    deep,
Saw fervid jewels sparkle in their sleep,

Saw glad gnomes working in the dusty
    light,
Saw great rocks crouching in the primal
    night.
I was drawn down, and after many days
Returned with stiller feet to walk the upper
    ways.

Song Made Flesh

I have no glory in these songs of mine:
  If one of them can make a brother strong,
It came down from the peaks of the divine—
  I heard it in the Heaven of Lyric Song.

The one who builds the poem into fact,
  He is the rightful owner of it all:
The pale words are with God's own power
    packed
  When brave souls answer to their bugle-
    call.

And so I ask no man to praise my song,
  But I would have him build it in his
    soul;
For that great praise would make me glad
    and strong,
  And build the poem to a perfect whole.

To High-born Poets

There comes a pitiless cry from the op-
    pressed—
A cry from the toilers of Babylon for their
    rest.—
O Poet, thou art holden with a vow:
The light of higher worlds is on thy brow,
And Freedom's star is soaring in thy breast.
Go, be a dauntless voice, a bugle-cry
In darkening battle when the winds are
    high—
A clear sane cry wherein the God is heard
To speak to men the one redeeming word.
    No peace for thee, no peace,
    Till blind oppression cease;
    The stones cry from the walls,
    Till the gray injustice falls—
Till strong men come to build in freedom-
    fate
The pillars of the new Fraternal State.

Let trifling pipe be mute,
Fling by the languid lute:
Take down the trumpet and confront the
    Hour,
And speak to toil-worn nations from a
    tower—
Take down the horn wherein the thunders
    sleep,
Blow battles into men—call down the fire—
The daring, the long purpose, the desire;
Descend with faith into the Human Deep,
And ringing to the troops of right a cheer,
Make known the Truth of Man in holy fear;
Send forth thy spirit in a storm of song,
A tempest flinging fire upon the wrong.

The Toilers

Their blind feet drift in the darkness, and no
one is leading;
Their toil is the pasture, where hyens and
harpies are feeding;
In all lands and always, the wronged, the
homeless, the humbled
Till the cliff-like pride of the spoiler is shaken
and crumbled,
Till the Pillars of Hell are uprooted and left
to their ruin,
And a rose-garden gladdens the places no rose
ever blew in,
Where now men huddle together and whisper
and harken,
Or hold their bleak hands over embers that
die out and darken.
The anarchies gather and thunder: few, few
are the fraters,
And loud is the revel at night in the camp of
the traitors. . . .

Say, Shelley, where are you—where are you?
    our hearts are a-breaking!
The fight in the terrible darkness—the shame
    —the forsaking!

The leaves shower down and are sport for
    the winds that come after;
And so are the Toilers in all lands the jest
    and the laughter
Of nobles—the Toilers scourged on in the
    furrow as cattle,
Or flung as a meat to the cannons that hunger
    in battle.

On the Gulf of Night

The world's sad petrels dwell for evermore
On windy headland or on ocean floor,
Or pierce the violent skies with perilous
    flights
That fret men in their palaces o' nights,
Breaking enchanted slumber's easeful boat,
With shudderings of their wild and dolorous
    note ;
They blow about the black and barren skies,
They fill the night with ineffectual cries.

There is for them not anything before,
But sound of sea and sight of soundless shore,
Save when the darkness glimmers with a ray,
And Hope sings softly, *Soon it will be day*.
Then for a golden space the shades are
    thinned,
And dawn seems blowing seaward on the
    wind.

But soon the dark comes wilder than before,
And swift around them breaks a sullen roar;
The tempest calls to windward and to lea,
And—they are seabirds on the homeless sea.

A Harvest Song

The gray bulk of the granary uplooms
    against the sky;
The harvest moon has dwindled—they have
    housed the corn and rye;
And now the idle reapers lounge against the
    bolted doors:
Without are hungry harvesters, within en-
    chanted stores.

Lo, they had bread while they were out a-toil-
    ing in the sun:
Now they are strolling beggars, for the har-
    vest work is done.
They are the gods of husbandry: they gather
    in the sheaves,
But when the autumn strips the wood, they're
    drifting with the leaves.

They plow and sow and gather in the glory
    of the corn ;
They know the noon, they know the pitiless
    rains before the morn ;
They know the sweep of furrowed fields that
    darken in the gloom—
A little while their hope on earth, then ever-
    more their tomb.

Two Taverns

I remember how I lay
On a bank a summer day,
Peering into weed and flower:
Watched a poppy all one hour;
Watched it till the air grew chill
In the darkness of the hill;
Till I saw a wild bee dart
Out of the cold to the poppy's heart;
Saw the petals gently spin,
And shut the little lodger in.

Then I took the quiet road
To my own secure abode.
All night long his tavern hung;
Now it rested, now it swung;
I asleep in steadfast tower,
He asleep in stirring flower;
In our hearts the same delight
In the hushes of the night;
Over us both the same dear care
As we slumbered unaware.

The Man under the Stone

When I see a workingman with mouths to
feed,
Up, day after day, in the dark before the
dawn,
And coming home, night after night, through
the dusk,
Swinging forward like some fierce silent
animal,
I see a man doomed to roll a huge stone up
an endless steep.
He strains it onward inch by stubborn inch,
Crouched always in the shadow of the
rock. . . .
See where he crouches, twisted, cramped,
misshapen !
He lifts for their life ;
The veins knot and darken—
Blood surges into his face. . . .

The Man under the Stone

Now he loses—now he wins—
Now he loses—loses—(God of my soul!)
He digs his feet into the earth—
There's a moment of terrified effort.   .   .   .
Will the huge stone break his hold,
And crush him as it plunges to the gulf?

The silent struggle goes on and on,
Like two contending in a dream.

Song to the Divine Mother *

Come, Mighty Mother, from the bright
  abode,
  Lift the low heavens and hush the Earth
    again;
Come when the moon throws down a shining
    road
  Across the sea—come back to weary men.

But if the moon throws out across the sea
  Too dim a light, too wavering a way,
Come when the sunset paves a path for Thee
  Across the waters fading into gray.

* This song should be read in the light of the deep and memorable truth that the Divine Feminine as well as the Divine Masculine Principle is in God—that he is Father-Mother, Two-in-One. It follows from this truth that the dignity of womanhood is grounded in the Divine Nature itself. The fact that the Deity is Man-Woman was known to the ancient poets and sages, and was grafted into the nobler religions of mankind. The idea is implied in the doctrine of the Divine Father, taught by our Lord in the Gospels; and it is declared in the first chapter of Genesis in the words: "God said, 'Let Us make man in Our image, after Our likeness.' . . . So God created man in His own image, in the image of God created He him; male and female created He them."

Dead nations saw Thee dimly in release—
  In Aphrodite rising from the foam :
Some glimmer of Thy beauty was on
    Greece,
  Some trembling of Thy passion was on
    Rome.

For ages Thou hast been the dim desire
  That warmed the bridal chamber of the
    mind :
Come burning through the heavens with
    Holy Fire,
  And spread divine contagion on mankind.

Come down, O Mother, to the helpless
    land,
  That we may frame our Freedom into
    Fate :
Come down, and on the throne of nations
    stand,
  That we may build Thy beauty in the
    State.

Song to the Divine Mother

Come shining in upon our daily road,
  Uphold the hero heart and light the mind;
Quicken the strong to lift the People's load,
  And bring back buried justice to mankind.

Shine through the frame of nations for a
    light,
  Move through the hearts of heroes in a
    song :
It is Thy beauty, wilder than the night,
  That hushed the heavens and keeps the
    high gods strong.

I know, Supernal Woman, Thou dost seek
  No song of man, no worship and no praise;
But thou wouldst have dead lips begin to
    speak,
  And dead feet rise to walk immortal ways.

Yet listen, Mighty Mother, to the child
  Who has no voice but song to tell his
    grief—
Nothing but tears and broken numbers wild,
  Nothing but woodland music for relief.

His song is but a little broken cry,
   Less than the whisper of a river reed;
Yet thou canst hear in it the souls that die—
   Feel in its pain the vastness of our need.

I would not break the mouth of song to tell
   My life's long passion and my heart's long
      grief,
But Thou canst hear the ocean in one shell,
   And see the whole world's winter in one
      leaf.

So here I stand at the world's weary feet,
   And cry the sorrow of the world's dumb
      years :
I cry because I hear the world's heart beat
   Weary of hope and broken through by tears.

For ages Thou hast breathed upon mankind
   A faint wild tenderness, a vague desire;
For ages stilled the whirlwinds of the mind,
   And sent on lyric seers the rush of fire.

And yet the world is held by wintry
    chain,
  Dead to Thy social passion, Holy One:
The dried-up furrows need the vital rain,
    The cold seeds the quick spirit of the
    sun.

Some day our homeless cries will draw Thee
    down,
    And the old brightness on the ways of
    men
Will send a hush upon the jangling town,
    And broken hearts will learn to love
    again.

Come, Bride of God, to fill the vacant
    Throne,
    Touch the dim Earth again with sacred
    feet;
Come build the Holy City of white stone,
    And let the whole world's gladness be
    complete.

Come with the face that hushed the heavens
    of old—
  Come with Thy maidens in a mist of
    light;
Haste for the night falls and the shadows
    fold,
  And voices cry and wander on the height.

The Flying Mist

I watch afar the moving Mystery,
The wool-shod, formless terror of the sea—
The Mystery whose lightest touch can
    change
The world God made to phantasy, death-
    strange.
Under its spell all things grow old and gray
As they will be beyond the Judgment Day.
All voices, at the lifting of some hand,
Seem calling to us from another land.
Is it the still Power of the Sepulcher
That makes all things the wraiths of things
    that were?

It touches, one by one, the wayside posts,
And they are gone, a line of hurrying ghosts.
It creeps upon the towns with stealthy feet,
And men are phantoms on a phantom
    street.

The Flying Mist

It strikes the towers and they are shafts of
    air,
Above the spectres passing in the square.
The city turns to ashes, spire by spire ;
The mountains perish with their peaks afire.
The fading city and the falling sky
Are swallowed in one doom without a cry.

It tracks the traveler fleeing with the gale,
Fleeing toward home and friends without
    avail ;
It springs upon him and he is a ghost,
A blurred shape moving on a soundless
    coast.
God ! it pursues my love along the stream,
Swirls round her and she is forever dream.
What Hate has touched the universe with
    eld,
And left me only in a world dispelled ?

From the Hand of a Child

One day a child ran after me in the street,
To give me a half-blown rose, a fire-white
    rose,
Its stem all warm yet from the tight-shut
    hand.
The little gift seemed somehow more to me
Than all men strive for in the turbid towns,
Than all they hoard up through a long wild
    life.
And as I breathed the heart-breath of the
    flower,
The Youth of Earth broke on me like a dawn,
And I was with the wide-eyed wondering
    things,
Back in the far forgotten buried time.
A lost world came back softly with the rose :
I saw a glad host follow with lusty cries
Diana flying with her maidens white,
Down the long reaches of the laureled hills.

Above the sea I saw a wreath of girls,
Fading to air in far-off poppy fields.
I saw a blithe youth take the open road :
His thoughts ran on before him merrily ;
Sometimes he dipped his feet in stirring
    brooks ;
At night he slept upon a bed of
    boughs. . .

This in my soul. Then suddenly a shape,
A spectre wearing yet the mask of dust
Jostled against me as he passed, and lo !
The jarring city and the drift of feet
Surged back upon me like the grieving sea.

At the Meeting of Seven Valleys

At the meeting of seven valleys in the west,
I came upon a host of silent souls,
Seated beside still waters on the grass.
It was a place of memories and tears—
Terrible tears.   I rested in a wood,
And there the bird that mourns for Itys
    sang—
Itys that touched the tears of all the world.
But climbing onward toward the purple
    peaks,
I passed, on silent feet, white multitudes,
Beyond the reach of peering memories,
Lying asleep upon the scented banks,
Their bodies burning with celestial fire.
A mighty awe came on me at the thought—
The strangeness of the beatific sleep,
The vision of God, the mystic bread of rest.

The Rock-Breaker

Pausing he leans upon his sledge, and
    looks—
  A labor-blasted toiler;
So have I seen, on Shasta's top, a pine
  Stand silent on a cliff,
Stript of its glory of green leaves and
    boughs,
  Its great trunk split by fire,
Its gray bark blackened by the thunder-
    smoke,
  Its life a sacrifice
To some blind purpose of the Destinies.

These Songs Will Perish

These songs will perish like the shapes of
    air—
The singer and the songs die out forever;
But star-eyed Truth (greater than song or
    singer)
Sweeps hurrying on: far off she sees a
    gleam
Upon a peak.   She cried to man of old
To build the enduring, glad Fraternal
    State—
Cries yet through all the ruins of the world—
Through Karnak, through the stones of
    Babylon—
Cries for a moment through these fading
    songs.

On wingèd feet, a form of fadeless youth,
She goes to meet the coming centuries,

And, hurrying, snatches up some human
    reed,
Blows through it once her terror-bearing
    note,
And breaks and throws away. It is enough
If we can be a bugle at her lips,
To scatter her contagion on mankind.

Printed in the United States
28447LVS00006B/242

9 781417 904808